ROBERT E. **WELLS** NEAC RBA

In Perspective

Ice Cream and Beer
oil on board 16 × 16 ins

CONTENTS

FOREWORD

Sara Cooper

Head of Collections
Towner Art Gallery

In this book, Robert E. Wells NEAC RBA shares his experience spanning his early interest in architecture to the more fluid forms of recent figurative art.

Wells is a Yorkshire-born painter, who studied in London, now living in East Sussex. Many people know him for his cityscape paintings, particularly around London, where unusual figure groupings and incidental traffic with brightly-coloured details are set against a strong architectural backdrop.

He worked for several years as an architectural illustrator, which you can see in many of his paintings, including the image opposite from the Towner Collection. It's just an ordinary entrance to a regular house in an Amsterdam street, but Wells' choice of what to capture is what makes it interesting. Rather than depicting the house as a complete architectural entity, he has focused on the arch that leads to the side door, with just a peek at the windows on the right. It is somehow more intriguing this way, and you can sense the artist's enjoyment in seeking out unusual views which encourages the viewer, in turn, to see places from a different perspective.

In recent years, his work has seen a shift from architecture to include more figurative elements, with complex multi-layered narratives, whilst retaining a freedom in paint application. He is increasingly inspired by the landscape, with atmospheric paintings of rural scenes. All of which you will see as you proceed through this book.

Wells regularly exhibits at the Royal Academy Summer Exhibition and is a member of the New English Art Club – a society that fits perfectly with Wells' interests and sensibilities. It's refreshing to see an artist with such an open and candid view of life and his work, and to witness in this book an unfolding story of self-expression.

Amsterdam Archway
oil on canvas 55 × 40 ins

Reproduced by kind permission
of the Towner Art Gallery

7

INTRODUCTION

Robert E. Wells

After leaving art college, I formed a band with a couple of friends. We were very enthusiastic, but totally ignorant as to what we were doing. Interesting ideas for songs would be started, abandoned and restarted, but without the expertise to properly construct them, they would be left in a state of disjointed chaos.

What I found surprising was the audience reaction to this. It was no great shock to see people ignoring us, or staring in astonishment at how bad we were, but very slowly there was a change. The same people, often musicians in other bands, would appear at different venues to watch us play. At first, I presumed it was to make fun of us, which made us slightly self-conscious. But after a while, we realised people were attracted to the strangeness of the set we played, and that our growing support was real.

The single biggest mistake in such a situation is to change. I figured that if people liked our music, they would *love* it with better structure. But the more we polished, the more audience numbers fell, and soon our promising little project had fallen apart. We had replaced charming naivety with slick professionalism and, in the process, lost the very strength that made us interesting.

The lessons learned would resonate later, and from the start of my life as a painter, it has constantly served as a warning of the dangers of losing your basic naïve response in much the same way as children eventually lose their ability to draw like a child.

Three Worshippers Outside San Giacometto
(see p.34)

Along the same lines, when putting this book together, I've tried not to over-polish it. I've resisted long descriptions proclaiming deeper meanings . . . Wherever possible, I prefer to let my work speak for itself.

ARCHITECTURAL

previous spread

The Houses of Parliament
(see p.28)

opposite

Eros
London
oil on canvas 36 × 36 ins

*The winning formula of wet pavement
and passing bus . . .*

Robert Wells' early paintings were understandably dominated by architectural themes. This was an artist playing to his strengths having worked as an architectural illustrator since leaving art college. Along with his firm grasp of composition, perspective, form and detail, he had also amassed many references over the years in sketchbooks – particularly of London.

He found a ready supply of clients during that period and he was introduced to the market through several London-based galleries keen to capitalise on his new work. Views of Eros, St Martin-in-the-Fields and Westminster were particularly successful, signalling the start of his transition from architectural illustrator to full-time artist.

St Mary Le Strand
London
oil on canvas 36 × 36 ins

Ever since his days as a Senior Associate at Joseph and Partners Architects in the late 1980s, Wells preferred to avoid public transport. Instead, he would walk from Waterloo station to West Central Street near Holborn every single day. Never without his sketchbook, he was constantly on the lookout for unusual vantage points. St Mary le Strand church being a particular favourite:

"I always thought it stood out nicely from the front, but when viewed from the rear on its awkward island in the middle of a busy road, it looks rather forgotten – cast permanently in shadow but somehow still managing to look eerily beautiful."

Breaking News

The Royal Courts of Justice, London

oil on canvas 36 × 36 ins

I had painted the Law Courts before. But adding the film crews that set up opposite during a newsworthy case changed the whole meaning of the painting. 'Breaking News' was the real drama – the big story of the day about to be replayed on the evening news channels.

St Martin-in-the-Fields

London

oil on canvas 14 × 18 ins

A view standing close to Trafalgar Square.

St Martin-in-the-Fields
London
oil on canvas 14 × 18 ins

A view from St Martin's Place.

Whitehall Towards Westminster
oil on canvas 24 × 24 ins

Barge with a Green Sail

Venice

oil on canvas 36 × 36 ins

A barge selling bric-a-brac, old furniture
and a familiar-looking painting.

Whitehall Towards Westminster
oil on canvas 24 × 24 ins

Red buses were a common inclusion in his earlier London works; the artist using these as a simple device for elevating mid-tonal ranged paintings. These proved rather popular and became, for a time, something of an accidental trademark:

"On a painting trip to my spiritual home in the North Yorkshire Moors, I was quite flattered to be approached by a nice couple who, familiar with my work, stopped to ask if I ever paint anything other than London . . ."

The Houses of Parliament
London
oil on board 5 × 9 ins

Contra-jour sketch study.

Parliament

London

oil on board 5 × 5 ins

Contra-jour sketch study
in preparation for a large studio oil.

Barge with a Green Sail

Venice

oil on canvas 36 × 36 ins

*A barge selling bric-a-brac, old furniture
and a familiar-looking painting.*

Churches were a frequent subject of Wells' architectural studies, but not just confined to London. He observed that San Giacometto in Venice had plenty in common with St Mary le Strand (see p.37):

"It also sits in a busy area – by the market, close to the Rialto Bridge. It is the oldest and arguably the most stunning church in the city. With its huge dominant clock face, it stands as one of Venice's most unusual buildings. And yet it sits lost behind the market stalls, barely receiving a passing glance."

The small sketch study (shown below) of three people standing outside before Mass was reworked as a larger studio work (opposite) to reveal more of the church, causing an interaction where both subjects seemed inextricably linked. This is a good example how Wells' treatment of subject was evolving, shifting towards more figurative and narrative themes.

Three Worshippers Outside San Giacometto (study)
oil on sketchbook paper, mounted on board 6 × 8 ins

Three Worshippers Outside San Giacometto

Venice

oil on canvas 14 × 18 ins

Porter in San Marco Square

Venice

oil on panel 16 × 16 ins

*The porters in their brightly-coloured rain macs scuttle
back-and-forth delivering produce directly from the barges.*

The Market Towards the Rialto Bridge

Venice

oil on panel 16 × 16 ins

*The constantly-busy market that leads from the Rialto Bridge
to the Fish Market dominates the view of one of Venice's
finest churches, San Giacometto, seen cropped in the
left-hand corner of the view.*

FIGURATIVE

Wells has always been intrigued by artworks that are difficult to summarise, or with ambiguous or conflicting narratives, and we can find these traits in many of his studio paintings:

"These are often formed from a variety of source materials. Sketchbook studies, photographs, memories and quotations would often materialise in no specific order. *The Fortune Teller* contained several such visual clues: parents and child, gypsy caravan, funfair ride . . . but the starting point was a hand-painted message on the outside of the caravan:

> *"What good I can do had best be done today.*
>
> *For such another golden chance you may wait in vain.*
>
> *Now is the time because I shall not pass this way again."*
>
> Gypsy Rose Lee, 1970

"I reread the sign many times over the years,
but as far as I know, she never moved from the spot."

Luca and Chiara

Eastbourne, East Sussex

oil on sketchbook paper, mounted
on board 6 × 6 ins

Our children sat on the living room window sill.

Preparing for a Walk

Bexhill seafront, East Sussex

oil on sketchbook paper, mounted
on board 6 × 8 ins

*Maria conducting a final inspection to
ensure all clothing is suitably fastened
prior to a bracing walk.*

Wells' family make frequent appearances in his recent works. In *The Piano, Red Blanket, The Homework Club and Sleeping Chiara* all is as it should be, with everyone presented in a natural home environment. But in others, their size and age are adapted to better suit the composition. In *Walking to the Shops and Luca and Chiara Playing in the Snow*, his children are depicted at a similar height, but without compromising the direct observation intended.

Preparing to Play

Rear garden, Eastbourne, East Sussex
oil on board 5 × 5 ins

Once again, Maria checks those all-important buttons and zips before allowing play to commence.

The Piano

Eastbourne, East Sussex

oil on panel 12 × 12 ins

(After Hopper)

An early evening oil study of the non-musical member of our family, Maria.

The Beer Garden

Whitby, North Yorkshire

oil on panel 12 × 12 ins

*"For us, the piece has both an optimistic, but also a sad
perspective. We love the affection shown to the child and dog,
but sense the loneliness and sadness conveyed too, particularly
in the demeanour of the father and the vulnerability of the
child's posture."*

**Extract from correspondence from Rosy and Steve shortly
after purchasing the painting.**

The Homework Club

Eastbourne, East Sussex

oil on canvas 36 × 36 ins

Maria, Chiara and Luca pondering a difficult maths homework question. The painting avoids truly depicting the terse exchange of opinions between mother and daughter.

Walking to the Shops

Carshalton Beeches, Sutton, South London

oil on panel 16 × 16 ins

*A cold but fresh day. Luca was far more interested in his
computer game than the snow-covered streets.*

above

Luca and Chiara Playing in the Snow

Eastbourne Pier, East Sussex

oil on sketchbook paper, mounted on board 6 × 8 ins

*A rare chance to build a snowman on the beach
adjacent to the pier. It was useful to have drawing
materials at hand as there was barely a trace of snow
left the following morning.*

below

Chiara and Sheep

Pevensey, East Sussex

oil on board 8 × 8 ins

A typical pose that Chiara would adopt. Arms and legs straight and centrally-balanced, directly facing the viewer.

opposite

The Red Blanket

South Downs, East Sussex

oil on panel 12 × 12 ins

Chiara, like her dad, can sit for hours silently contemplating on the hills above our house in any weather – a blanket and flask of tea in hand.

Sleeping Chiara

Hotel in Montparnasse, Paris

oil on panel 8 × 12 ins

An oil sketch influenced by a Vuillard at the Orsay Museum,
which I consider to be the finest gallery in Europe. I am always
amazed how quiet it can be. Presumably thanks to the Louvre
for absorbing most of the passing trade.

The Quiet Walk Home

Barnes, South West London
oil on panel 12 × 12 ins

*At night, the passageways around
Barnes Station are a foreboding contrast
to the pleasant leafy village by day.*

Beach Volleyball
Belvedere, Southern Italy
oil on canvas 16 × 16 ins

Often, the artist's work is simply a reaction to natural settings, serving no great purpose other than to record a situation on a particular day. His wife is from Napoli, so the Wells family often travel to Italy, and *Beach Volleyball* was painted on one such visit.

"There is a town called Belvedere in the south which is jewel-like on the surface. However, one evening while painting people playing and relaxing on the beach, I noticed that right next to them, there was an open sewage pipe leading straight into the sea. In Italy, they can be very strict about some aspects of society and yet overlook situations outsiders might find difficult to comprehend. The contrast between beauty and ugliness in such situations can be quite intriguing."

Regent's Park

London

oil on sketchbook paper, mounted on board 6 × 6 ins

An old man sunbathing on a park bench
next to the boating lake.

Regent's Park is a sketch painted on a family trip to London:

"The original sketch was rectangular and included a young, pretty girl eating a sandwich. She was sat on the same bench as the old man in shorts, socks and shoes. Neither person seemed aware of the other, and yet from my vantage point, they seemed a very strange and uncomfortable pairing."

Wherever he goes, Wells always makes a point of recording such sightings, no matter how trivial they may seem. Some sketches, such as *The Wrong Shorts, Siblings* and *Two Boys* (see p.69, 70 & 73) are earmarked for larger studio painting development. Whereas others are destined to remain as reference material, at least for the time being . . .

The Wrong Shorts

Sangineto, Southern Italy

Sketchbook paper, mounted on board 6 × 8 ins

One size does not fit all, or so it would seem.

RA Summer Exhibition 2014

The Siblings
Filey, North Yorkshire
oil on panel 8 × 8 ins

The boy on the right made me smile, looking every
bit as uncomfortable as me on holiday.

RA Summer Exhibition 2018

above

Preliminary sketch for Two boys
Sangineto, Southern Italy
graphite on postcard 4 × 6 ins

opposite

Two Boys
Sangineto, Southern Italy
oil on panel 6 × 6 ins

*Two awkward-looking boys
in the communal swimming pool.*

The family often accompany Wells whilst gathering visual information in the form of sketchbooks, oil studies and photography.

Occasionally patience is tested [see *Maria* p.78/79] but other times they contribute their own personal ideas which may form the basis for future projects.

On a recent visit to Leeds, a trip to the pub turned into a photoshoot for *The Departed*, *Waiting for Friends* and *Walkway*, with the children taking photographs and arranging one another to seek out the most dramatic compositions to comunicate an appropriate dialogue. Wherever possible, they are actively encouraged to be collaborators, to observe their surroundings carefully and to engage with the the mechanics of the creative process. This not only helps Wells see things from an alternative angle, but also – as he says – "hopefully allows them to take something away each time which might be a useful resource to apply in their own life journeys".

The Departed
oil on sketchbook paper 12 × 8 ins

The location for this painting was the "The Highland" pub in Leeds. Once in a crowded area of tightly-packed terraced housing it now stands completely alone, bleak but defiant, a suitable backdrop to receive the painful news of a pending breakup.

below

Waiting for Friends

oil on sketchbook paper 8 × 6 ins

*Chiara modelling on the walkway tower
adjacent to the Leeds Inner Ring Road.*

opposite

Walkway

oil on canvas 36 × 48 ins

Luca on the inner staircase of the walkway tower.

BLACK & WHITE
DRAWING

Maria

Sangineto, Southern Italy

pencil on sketchbook paper 6 × 8 ins

Sketch study inscribed, '12.15am. 13th Aug. Maria Reading.'
Or to be more accurate, Maria bored and almost asleep,
waiting for me to:

a) finish my sketch
b) finish my beer

Maria

Sangineto, Southern Italy

pencil on sketchbook paper 8 × 8 ins

Another sketch study, drawn on the same trip, with the
subject marginally more awake.

"Sketchbooks underpin everything."

Sometimes his sketches find a life of their own, directly leading on to a studio painting. But broadly, Wells makes no deliberate attempt to see every drawing as useful, beyond just recording a specific subject. He finds this relieves the pressure of trying to succeed with every drawing.

This was very different to working on architectural concept drawings, where accuracy and portraying just the right atmosphere were vital to a successful outcome.

There needed to be clear boundaries regarding what the drawing had to achieve, and how it would relate to other aspects of a presentation. But no matter how restrictive the brief, it was still important that each work had a freshness and authoritative swagger, and that every project should be approached with the same enthusiasm on every occasion.

above

Dome
Saint Petersburg
pen and ink wash 6 × 6 ins

*Concept sketch for redevelopment area
adjacent to the railway station.*

**Reproduced by kind permission of Larry Malcic,
Design Principal, HOK, London**

opposite

Saint Petersburg
ink drawing on tracing paper 8 × 12 ins

*Feasibility sketch study for the redevelopment
of Saint Petersburg.*

**Reproduced by kind permission of Larry Malcic,
Design Principal, HOK, London**

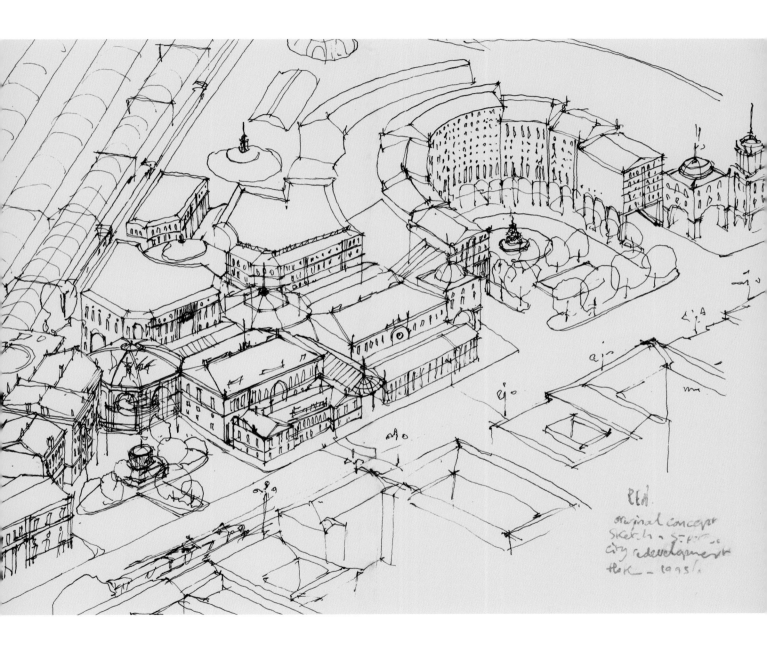

REH.
original concept
sketch - g- fit -
city redevelopment
the ____ 1995.

The Printworks

Manchester

graphite on tracing paper, mounted on board 16 × 16 ins

Early black-and-white concept sketch for the Printworks.
The brief: "When Batman met Blade Runner".

Reproduced by kind permission of David Gester, Vice President, RTKL,
Architects for the Printworks project, Manchester

Prior to the advances in computerised design, the role of the perspective artist was hugely important. Wells remembers, "If you were lucky enough to possess a technique that could convincingly articulate a space in a flattering light, you could expect to be very busy."

He was usually selected for pencil sketches or ink line drawings for interior and exterior spaces. His pencil work tended to be very quick emotive concept sketches, as an easy, cost-effective way to test client reaction before progressing too far. His ink drawings were far more detailed and intensely drawn – usually on tracing paper, so lines could be gently erased using a sharp razor blade if alterations were needed. They were usually set in natural surroundings, with portrayals of people going about their daily business. If cars were shown, they had to be the correct make and model. All this served to give an air of convincing accuracy to the design. Transferred onto card, the print would then be suitable for watercolour rendering. Wells' drawings proved to be very persuasive marketing tools and were often the centrepiece of major design schemes, offering an opportunity to see everything in three dimensions for the first time. As a result, they helped to initiate huge building design projects and were a pivotal tool in generating the necessary finances.

Toucan

London Zoo

pencil on tracing paper,
mounted on board 6 × 6 ins

LANDSCAPE

previous spread

Sheep

Pevensey, East Sussex

oil on canvas 10 × 16 ins

*The fields behind Pevensey Castle are a nice quiet area
to paint without being disturbed.*

opposite

Cow

Willingdon, Eastbourne, East Sussex

oil on sketchbook paper, mounted on board 6 × 6 ins

*Painted in the fields close to home, this large dairy cow
was oblivious to the flood water that had recently formed,
virtually surrounding her.*

Wells' father was a relief driver for the mobile Midland Bank based in Whitby. His job was to drive around the Yorkshire Moors and rendezvous at certain places to allow farmers and local people in isolated communities access to banking. Although not technically allowed, a young Robert Wells often went along and would be dropped in one village and told to walk to the next to meet up. This meant walking long distances and spending considerable amounts of time alone. To occupy himself, he started to keep a diary, which later became full of drawings and proved to be the start of his long-term relationship with sketchbook use.

Four Sheep and a Lamb

Goathland, North Yorkshire Moors

oil on board 8 × 8 ins

As a boy, the sight of the long-since demolished 'Golf Balls' at the huge RAF Fylingdales Early Warning Station were the highlight of any visit, looking like pure science fiction. Nowadays, I consider this to be one of the most beautiful places on Earth. It feels like home from home.

Frozen Fields

South Downs National Park, East Sussex

oil on board 12 × 12 ins

Painted in the early evening of a very cold day, with clear skies and the promise of a quickly-forming and bitter night frost.

Three Cows
Pevensey, East Sussex
Oil on panel 12 × 12 ins

The artist's current home is on the edge of the South Downs National Park in East Sussex, so there is no shortage of inspiring landscape right on his doorstep.

"There is a field that is home to the most splendid herd of Black Hereford cows I have ever seen.

Their markings are completely black except for their white faces. They have an almost gothic strangeness about them and, coupled with their rather curious nature, they can be rather intimidating. The first time I painted them, I became quite engrossed and was unaware that some had quietly formed a semi-circle behind me, quietly observing me at work. I was able to move away without a problem, but they had really startled me. I have since found a great vantage point where a stream cuts through the field. I am far more relaxed at a safe distance – with me on one side and my curious art-loving friends on the other."

The Herd
Pevensey, East Sussex
oil on sketchbook paper, mounted on board 6 × 8 ins

Cow Face

Pevensey, East Sussex
heavily-layered oil paint on sketchbook paper,
mounted on board 6 × 8 ins

*This particular old girl had such an interesting,
characterful face. She reminded me of what
Rembrandt's cow might look like . . .
not that he ever possessed a cow, as far
as we know.*

Amsterdam
gouache on board 8 × 12 ins

It was pouring with rain, so this had to be mainly repainted in the studio due to water damage. If you look carefully in the bottom left corner, there is a reflection of someone wearing red shoes. They seemed totally fascinated by the painting taking shape. I have been back to Amsterdam numerous times and have not been able to locate either the doorways or the archway painting owned by the Towner Gallery. (p.6) I never realised it was so easy to lose things there.

BIOGRAPHY

Robert E. Wells is a Yorkshire-born artist, known for his cityscape paintings as well as rural landscapes and figurative works. A member of the New English Art Club and the Royal Society of British Artists, he regularly exhibits his work in solo shows and the RA Summer Exhibition.

QUESTIONABLE CAREER ADVICE

From an early age, as the only boy and youngest of four children, Wells instinctively knew he wanted to be an artist. His school careers advisors, however, were quick to pour scorn on this idea, insisting that his lack of academic prowess meant that an apprenticeship as an electrician, plumber or builder would be a better fit.

Thankfully, he did not heed this advice. He enrolled at the local art college where one of his lecturers encouraged him to learn 3D drawing techniques in case they would be useful at some point in his career.

THE ARCHITECTURAL ILLUSTRATOR YEARS

After college, he worked long hours as a junior designer at an architectural practice, whilst playing in a band at night. This exhausting schedule soon made him realise that he needed to decide between design and music. A job offer to work as an interior designer in Kuwait helped make the decision. Upon his return to the UK, he found work with a succession of design-based employers, which eventually led to him setting up as a specialist freelance architectural illustrator.

As he became more established, he started getting more and more work in London, with clients including HOK and RTKL. At first, he commuted on a weekly basis from Leeds, treating every visit as a sketching exercise – walking for miles around the capital recording anything and everything of interest. "It all seemed so vibrant and totally compelling," he recalls.

LONDON CALLING

He finally moved to London in 1998, settling in Barnes, after being offered the position of Senior Associate at Joseph and Partners – one of London's oldest architectural practices. In order to keep him out of mischief, they funded a part-time MA in *The Illustration and Rendering of Architectural Spaces* which he completed in little over a year.

Further employment came as Senior Visualiser at Harrods in Knightsbridge, and it was around this time that Wells began working on small oils, as well as his usual sketchbooks. He had already enjoyed some success at the RA Summer Exhibition, but it was in 2002 that he really started to find his feet as a full-time artist.

THE JOY OF RED DOTS

The New Grafton Gallery in Barnes contacted Wells about exhibiting in their Christmas show. He supplied around six paintings, all of views around London, and sat back for an agonising wait . . .

"The surprise and relief at seeing a red dot appear next to one painting after another was so exciting and is still a highlight of my working life as an artist."

BIOGRAPHICAL DETAILS

Born Albert Road, Morley, Leeds

1973-76	Batley School of Art
1976-84	Designer, Architectural Interiors
1984-2002	Architectural Perspective Artist
1988	Cert Ed, HollyBank, Yorkshire
	Moved to Barnes, S W London
	Senior Associate, Joseph and
	Partners Architects
	MA. The Illustration and Rendering of
	Architectural Spaces, University of London
1992	MA, University of East London
2002	Moved to Eastbourne, East Sussex

SOCIETY MEMBERSHIPS

New English Art Club (NEAC)
Royal Society of British Artists (RBA)
Fellow of Chartered Society of Designers (FCSD)

PRIZES AND AWARDS

2014, 2017	The Davison Award for Oil Painting, RBA
2016	Frinton Frames Award, RBA
2012	The Howard de Walden Art Prize (First)
2007	Daler-Rowney Prize
2006	President's Choice, RBA

PAST EXHIBITIONS

2017	Signet Contemporary Art
2015	Royal Automobile Club
2013	Brian Sinfield Gallery
2008-09	Walker Art Gallery
2007	Whittington Fine Art
2007	W. H. Patterson Gallery
2006	Fairfax Gallery, Chelsea
2002-05	New Grafton Gallery

GROUP SHOWS

2017	Thompson's Gallery
2014	Panter & Hall
2014	Llewellyn Alexander Gallery

REGULAR EXHIBITOR AT:

RA Summer Exhibition
NEAC Annual Exhibition
RBA Annual Exhibition

PUBLIC COLLECTIONS

Towner Art Gallery
Pannett Art Gallery and Museum

PUBLICATIONS

2016 (Oct-Nov edition) International Artist,
The Power of the Sketchbook
2014 Royal Academy illustrated catalogue (p87)
2014 (Feb-Mar edition) International Artist,
an Architectural Perspective (p96-102)
2014 (Jan edition) The Artist, Masterclass (p12-15)
2005 (Jan edition) The Artist, In Conversation (p46-47)

TELEVISION

28 Sept 2017 London Live, interview

Waiting
Napoli, Italy
oil on board 8 × 8 ins

Napoli, the birthplace of my wife Maria,
seen here with Luca, waiting for a storm to pass.

ACKNOWLEDGEMENTS

I would like to thank Graham Rees – graphic design, Barry O'Donovan – biography, Douglas Atfield – photography and Onder Sadet – website design, for their professional expertise in the making of this book.

Further thanks to Sara Cooper for her foreword, Larry Malcic and David Gester for allowing permission to reproduce sketches for their architectural design projects.

Finally to the clients and galleries who have provided invaluable support for my work over the years, without them I would not have been able to persue such a rewarding career.

I am so grateful.
Robert E. Wells, July 2018.

Foreword © Sara Cooper
Introduction © Robert E. Wells
Biography © Barry O'Donovan
Images © Robert E. Wells

Design by Graham Rees Design
Printed by Graphius, Belgium

Published by Rewind Books, in Great Britain 2018
ISBN 978-1-5272-2703-3